CONNOR & SEAL

Sibling Rivalry Press, LLC
PO Box 26147
Little Rock, AR 72221

info@siblingrivalrypress.com

www.siblingrivalrypress.com

ISBN: 978-1-943977-75-8

Library of Congress Control Number: 2019953150

By special invitation, this title is housed in the Rare Book and Special Collections Vault of the Library of Congress.

First Sibling Rivalry Press Edition, March 2020

CONNOR & SEAL
a harlem story in 47 poems

JEE LEONG KOH

SIBLING RIVALRY PRESS

DISTURB/ENRAPTURE

Little Rock, Arkansas

for Guy

Two strings, one pierced cry.
So many ways to imitate
The ringing in his ears.

—Rita Dove, *Thomas and Beulah*

Contents

Seal

Timeline

1983   Seal is born in Kingston, Jamaica, on Love Street.

1990   Connor is born in Nebraska City, Nebraska. His brother Tom was born four years earlier in 1986.

1999   Connor's father moves out and the parents divorce subsequently.

2003   Seal moves to New York City to study business at Columbia University. He rents a room in Harlem.

2006   Connor moves to New York City and studies English and Art History. He attends a coming-out support group at Identity House.

2007   Seal is hired at Houlihan Lokey Investment Bank as a financial analyst. He finds an apartment in Chelsea.

2010   Connor and Seal meet at an 80's Dance Party. Connor has just been hired as a grant writer by Orpheus Dance Theater.

2011   Seal leaves boyfriend Brad for Connor.

2012   Connor tours China with Orpheus Dance Theater.

2016   Connor is hired by the Studio Museum in Harlem. Connor and Seal move to Harlem, to 122nd Street, beside Marcus Garvey Park. In November, Donald Trump is elected as the 45th President of the United States.

2017   Connor participates in the Women's March on Washington, a day after Trump's inauguration.

2019   Connor and Seal visit Seal's family in Kingston for the first and only time.

2020   Connor and Seal marry at City Hall.

2025   Tom dies at the age of 39. He is savagely beaten to death by a stranger he had sex with.

2029   Connor brings boy bot Newton home.

2036   First mass protest against social inequities at Central Park (Fourth of July). Police fires into the protest, killing 12 people. Seal provides information to the Feds in the subsequent security operation to detain and question undesirable social elements.

2040   A pipe bomb goes off at the Masque Ball in Apollo Theater. A domestic terrorist group called Demos claims responsibility.

2041   The United States invades Syria.

2046   Second mass protest at Central Park on the tenth anniversary of Bloody Fourth.

2051   Newton is decommissioned.

2053   The United States withdraws its troops from Syria, finally beaten by the local guerillas aided by the Russians and the Chinese. Seal retires and begins teaching at the Barron Trump School for the Gifted.

2054   Connor sees the First Emperor of China show at the Met Museum.

2056   Third mass protest at Central Park on the twentieth anniversary of Bloody Fourth.

2064   Seal dies of chronic ischaemic heart disease at the age of 81.

2066   Connor dies at the age of 76 of a mysterious new virus.

Connor

"The wine-flushed, bold-eyed boys, and even the girls,
Devoured her with their eager, passionate gaze..."

—Claude McKay, "The Harlem Dancer"

Nebraska

From the bluff
we turned our backs on the river
and opened a trail
as Lewis and Clark.

We spotted the grizzly,
Tom did, glummer than Meriwether,
and gave him wide berth
slowly on our stomachs.

When I hit
some raccoon shit, Tom changed
my name to Pvt. John Collins,
tied my paws to a tree,

whipped me with the switch
of a branch,
rubbing his orange until he shot
gum.

We hurried home, it was getting dark,
and watched dad slam the boot
on boxes of his stuff
and drive off.

I was the one to break
the silence, kept up during the whipping—
Tom, let's go back
and tie me up.

Art Show at the Center

On a black dummy,
a shawl—not cashmere,
cigarette butts.

Apple seeds arranged
into tea cozies
around the ankles of trees.

So this is what art is!

You are one thing and you
are used for another.

The Artist-in-Residence
flashes me
a smile, showing her
New York lights.

The star of the show:

cheap yellow soap—three blocks,
height of my chest,
voluptuous sculptures
of urinals.

The urge to use them!
Spray them
and still be clean.

Use them up.

A Tale of Two Cities, Three Maybe
(with apologies to Jon Ims and Trisha Yearwood)

She's a baby from Vietnam,
from Saigon, if the truth be told,
She's a girl from Nebraska City
and sixteen years old.
She's unusual, that's for sure.
She's askin' him out for ice cream
at Nancy's Old Fashioned Ice Cream Parlor
by Dick's Drive-In.

She's in love with the boy
She's in love with the boy
but after a whole year of eatin' pussy
he knows he ain't in love with Katie.

She's smart as a whip,
a head turner, a head spinner, a looker,
but he has eyes only
for her quarterback brother.
In the lab, she makes up excuses
to peek at his dissection.
He sneaks his looks in the locker room
at Scott's pink ass and Joe's erection.

She's in love with the boy
She's in love with the boy
but after a whole year of eatin' pussy
he knows he ain't in love with Katie.

He tells her at Farm Aid
he's applyin' to New York University
This town's too small for big dreams,
he complains, to let her down easy.

With her ma's heart condition,
she ain't goin' anywhere.
Trisha Yearwood looks so small on stage
as her voice choppers into the air:

She's in love with the boy.
She's in love with the boy
but after a whole year of suckin' boner
she knows she's been conned by Conner.

Arrival New York

Shirtless bartenders
popping the cork.
Drag queens hosting
Devil's Pitchfork.
Derrick, Sam, Alberto, Jee,
can such places be?

Flirtations flit.
Beauty meets.
Grown men deep
kissing on the streets.
Derrick, Sam, Alberto, Jee,
can such places be?

Talk we must about
coming out
in the calmness of
Identity House.
Derrick, Sam, Alberto, Jee,
can such places be?

Can such places be
for good?
They feel too good.
A neighborhood,
Derrick, Sam, Alberto, Jee,
can such places be?

80's Dance Party on Throwback Thursday

It is time to bring your face into focus
before this lens moves below the chin to other features harder
to identify as yours.
The best image is that of the cheeks.

The right cheek and the left cheek do not meet.
Like the back of the hand and the palm,
like the head of a silver coin and its tail,
the cheeks do not see each other except in a mirror or a photograph.

This is true of my cheeks
until your right brushes my left when we dance and, in that flash of flesh,
the coin turns up both head and tail,
the back of the hand shakes hands with the palm.

Later, at the Same Dance Party

Finally he withdraws

    his sweet body

        from the kiss, and the veil descends.

I'm completely

involved with someone,   *he's coming back*

    tomorrow.

    Thrust together by his words,

        we taste

each other's mouth

    through the silk

and all the names of the world   body   kiss   tomorrow

    his name Seal

        swaddle in a moist

  napkin

      the things they designate.

When he backs off yet again,

          a cry

I cannot recognize

      passes my lips,
              Take me home with you.

It does not cross the field of the cloth of gold.

    He presses

through the crushed

        bodies,

    pulling his tee-shirt down

             as he goes.

Cocktail Napkins

He's not on Grindr or other hook-
up apps, but he's on LinkedIn,
steel blue jacket, snowy shirt, grey tie,
Columbia cuff links.

Winter changes
into spring,
messages grow into meetings,
coffees, then happy
hour drinks,

closeness closing
in in
spite of our differences I tally
on cocktail napkins.

Seal	Connor
Kingston, Jamaica	Nebraska City, Nebraska
28 (not too old)	21
oldest of 7	younger of 2 boys
financial analyst	grant writer (first job!)
music	art, theater, dance, music, reading
ackee and saltfish	pork chops
aqua vitae (whiskey)	lychee martini

And the difference that seals
the deal, as he
puts it, with a wicked
glint,
he's a bull top and I'm a bottom.
Win-win.

Song

He's no bull top.
He's thin, Big Seal
and Little Seal.

He's a bull, top
of the shelf, in
the china shop.

Thin as a string,
two strings, and I
play his Orpheus.

He's my bull top,
and I am his
silly bucket.

Hi Harlem

Now we live high enough, above surrounding roofs,
to see the unimpeded sky turn ever so slowly to light,
the black church tower coming into sight with its bell,
turn in the spring evening to purple wash, into which
the water tank, like a squat rocket, catapults its icon
and flies without moving as darkness falls around it,
the shopping mall pulsating in the corner of the eye
with an unearthly glow, high enough to see all this,
unimpeded, I repeat, with only the purple looking in,
when the buzz-cut jock in the clip, left hand relaxed
on the wheel, master hand on his tiny stick, looking
back and forth between the motorway and her activity
between her legs, passing pylons and twelve-wheelers,
brings himself off, oh my god, self-recording, laughing.

Was It Known as Mount Morris Then?

You used to live in Harlem,
back in the noughts,
and cruised the boys in the outdoor pool
to the north of the park.
Not in the sex clubs,
which you compare to shooting fish in a barrel.
I can see you
chatting up a young buck, one yourself,
while children thrashed about on floats and parents
shouted directions,
then heading for the changing room,
you first, and then your trick,
to dry off.

I can't wait for summer,
if the boys at the gym are anything
to go by,
when the pool will be filled with water
and the park with the sour cherry,
which the website tells me is
self-pollinating.

The Morning after Trump's Election (Watusi)

How to paint the morning after?
The bed holds my hands down.
I'll soon be jobless.

How to paint the morning after
when America's business
is again business?

How to paint the morning? After
Alma Thomas who painted,
after Henri Matisse,

how to paint. The morning, after
Obama's golden snail,
belongs to the blue dancers of Watusi.

How? To paint the morning after,
to stand the snail on its feet,
turn Matisse ninety degrees.

I Don't Believe in the Long Arc of Justice

In the Martin Luther King Jr. Senior Center,
a dozen Martins and Martinas doze and drool
in front of the Baptist preacher on cable TV.
They know better than to take him seriously.

Sure, they sometimes wake at night, blurred
with heat and sweat, and cry out for a savior.
But in their better, which means less fearful,
moments, they see through cataracts the truth.

No one will save them from slow deterioration
or a heart attack. No words will do. Sure, it is
far far better to have brave words than harsh,
but the time for words is almost over, so they

look forward to their children coming for them,
after a hard day's slog, to bundle them into coats
and wheel the feebler out to the open chariot,
paid for by monthly installments and rough hands.

Returning from the Women's March in DC

Reached the top
of the subway stairs

when a scream swivels
all heads to the corner deli.

An Amazon
swinging with amazing force another girl
to the ground,

then kneeing her sternum,
punching her eyes—

her sistah kicks the side
of the head, once, twice.

Should I help, I think, and then
another thought

swings up,
laughing mirthlessly into the sun,

she must have done
something to deserve the thrashing,

tried to mount her boy
or talked trash behind her back.

Rough
justice.

I turn my own corner,
black as the watchful street.

Sisters Caribbean Cuisine

They are an allegory, these two women,
chicory brown between the flaming red
of their origami turbans and long dresses.
They move with a stateliness that owns
a required quickness for plucking a child
from a river or flower from a prickly stem.
They have a brother (husband?), succulent
as goat curry, collard greens, candied yam,

who's not always there. They do without him.
Once, a rock flew through the window
and made off with the register. Empty,
a sister disclosed as she swept up the glass.
(One speaks English, the other doesn't.)
Restaurant's on the rough side of the park.

Ackee and Saltfish

He took it into his head,
his mama says,
he was a seal
after watching National Geographic

and so we called him Seal.
I predicted he would head north
for the chill.

She looks so happy, heliotropic,
to have him back and to welcome
his *bredren*.

We're eating his favorite breakfast,
ackee and salted cod,
made the unique way mama knows

in his family home on Love Street,
which runs parallel to Crooks Street.

Mind you, mama says,
it's not a hard dish to make,

but mind you,
the unopened fruit is toxic.

Under the Elevated Railway Tracks

In the plant nursery a muscular Chinese man
balances on his right hand a tray of miniatures
as he walks among the cactuses and hyacinths
in the rumbling shadow of the scheduled trains.
He brings me back to Kunming, the acrobats
climbing up one another, the strongest lifting
clear the other two, a trinity exerting pressure
at every point and achieving a momentary rest.

I see him and I see you look at him, his shorts
snug, round, and covered in a pattern of ferns,
his big arm lifting the potted plants for home.
You walk ahead to peek back at his face, I
following. A good face, strong-jawed and open.
Love, do you hear somebody call out for Adam?

Tom's a-cold

Hooked up
to a machine, not a tree,
I am thrashed again by Tom's boyish avatar.

Poor Tom,
hid behind Barb and the kids
and died, a year this day, of time's leather hiding.

The cock-
y grin brightening the glum face,
the muscles studying their clout. Sir, permission

to come.
The manager, a boy bot,
releases me from the buckles but not the dream.

Eyes green
like Tom's, clean-shaven desert.
I can't stop myself from holding out my heart for him.

Between
my paws, he bends his head, cool
and debonair steel under the mess of real hair.

New Boy in the House

He is of Greek design
but they call him Newton—
for every action there is
an equal etc..

Seal hates him, the way he sucks
up to me, shadows me
to show openings, and
sides with me in our
long-running arguments.

When I stay out late
again, for an AI
party, getting artificially
inseminated
by a drone of droids,

I come home
and see them cuddling in bed
like a question mark,

which I answer
by joining in.

They move to admit me,
Newton
in the middle.

We sleep until the old unruly sun
wakes us up
with morning reactions.

Our household
also follows
the laws of thermo(nuclear)
dynamics.

Yellow Leaves (Turing)

A. The sonnet "That time of year" by William Shakespeare, what number is it?

B. It's Sonnet 73.

A. In the second line "When yellow leaves, or none, or few, do hang," would not "red leaves" do as well or better?

B. It wouldn't scan.

A. How about "dying leaves"? It would scan all right.

B. It wouldn't be as visual and yet evocative.

A. What do you mean?

B. Yellow is the color of butter, traffic lights, daffodils, all good things, but yellow is also the color of aging, like human skin. "Yellow leaves" shows us good things dying.

A. But why "yellow leaves, or none, or few" in that order? Isn't it more logical to have "yellow leaves, or few, or none"?

B. To have "few" at the end is sadder than to have "none." Haven't you seen balding men combing the last few strands across their scalp?

A. Yes, I've seen them. I've sworn never to do that.

B. Good for you.

A. I love the line "Bare ruined choirs, where late the sweet birds sang." It's so musical.

B. It's the most beautiful line of the sonnet. But isn't it a flaw of the sonnet? To have the most beautiful line so early that the rest of the sonnet never quite lives up to it?

A. I've never thought of that.

B. It just occurred to me.

A. Maybe it comes early because beauty comes early, when we are young. Then it's gone.

B. I see.

A. This thou, Connor, perceiv'st, which makes thy love more strong—

B. To love that well which thou, Newton, must leave ere long.

Apollo

The evening of the blast,
the museum was open
and you were saying, *what a shitty day*
you had at the Exchange.

The shock blew apart all the glass,
and your voice on the phone
grew small and indistinct
and then—nothing.

Through black and space and safety,
I flew in a silver capsule,
fired by the archer-god
so bright I had to look away.

Your voice, coming over
like a radio transmission,
Connor, speak to me
drifted the ship back to land.

I stepped out in a daze.
Earth that night
had the look and step and devastation
of the moon.

Newton

When do you pull the plug on your robot?
His lovely face unlined, the best upgrades
you have the money for, notwithstanding,
they won't support his model any more.

He cannot express any wish but yours,
so fixed his trust that it approaches love,
it *is* love, infinite abandonment,
his utmost substance for your highest will.

No running down to naught. No delegate,
no substitute, will do what I must do.
No turning a blind eye to darkening eyes.

Instead, a party in his favorite gear,
to bed and vows, before I pull the plug—
you're loved, you're loved, you will not disappear.

Handheld Devices

Short Straw

Why don't we have any
A-list friends, you spit
and stick your purple
toothbrush aslant my
Oral-B, blue, bristling.

Science Fiction

In the 2(x)ist
underwear I bought
for your birthday you
sighed in our cot,
I woke up in Paris.

Stored Value

Before my MoMA
card expires, I will
top up my plastic
bottle with Perrier.

Running Shoes

Everything slows.
The eyes. The brain.
Even your heart
but for the electrodes.

Quality Care

Don't slip and fall
on the Furniture
Polish I over-
sprayed to the floor,
smelling of lemons.

Strongman from Qinshi Huangdi's Tomb

The head would have given the final expression
like a peacock's tail feathers, had we not lost it,
and yet the body is too strongly modeled for us
to require a face. Rounded like high cheekbones,

the shoulders weigh two brawny arms, snakes
lashing within, holding what would have been
a great bendy pole, with a colleague, on which
an acrobat would swing and somersault and land.

Driven to the ground but rising from his feet,
the enormous torso, of earth once trampled on
by trumpeting beasts, is not smooth like a smile
but frowns with clear cracks, in large fragments,

about the roof of the barbarous belly, the lines,
opening and closing, emanating from our mouth.

Counting Song

This is failing territory, where we will die
of prostate cancer or sweet pneumonia,
after we hang our coats in the broom closet.
This old man plays nick nack on my drum.

Ambition, the devil, has descended to details
and every meal is eaten with Dissatisfaction.
Give, my Love, the long-dead dog a bone.
Paddy whacked, this old man comes rolling home.

Friends go before us—who knows where.
The bell rings for other men, our door
opens to the mocking grin of thinning air.
This old man plays nick nack on my shoe.

Look, our eyesight is deserting us. Parody!
They say hearing, HEARING, the first to go.
Sans eyes, sans ears, sans smell, sans taste,
paddy whacked, this old man comes rolling home.

What have we left? The furniture of memory.
Dining table your dad made, the ghostly TV,
the ghastly licks of animal horn on the wall.
This old man plays nick nack on my tree.

Residence of sadness where we intend joy,
it will be a property, a prop, for tired feet.
After the drill square and the stroll garden,
paddy whacked, this old man comes rolling home.

Elegy for Seal

Black light, black light,
as still as the black train
is frantic, rushing the
black night. As narrow
as the black boulevard
is wide. Old as Cheops
and as the black olive
is young, blasted time.
Frequent as injustice
and as rare as equal
understanding. Sexy
as hell and as heaven
is detumescent. Tiny
as he, snorting, was big
inside after his white
boy had first opened
me up. As strong as
the curtains are weak.
As quiet as the siren
is alarming, arresting
never the black river.

The Classical Theater of Harlem

Downstage left, enter the Self in the making
of what we all must see, the busy and free crayon,
the things you can do with a piece of string,
then it gets called names, it calls others names,
one name rising above the others to stand for
the Self's self, for whom it makes a bouquet
of involuntary thought and ventures beyond
the orchard, listening in the wing for the place
to come back on stage, for it loves the stage,
the strutting and the fretting, the figure it cuts
with its kitchen scissors around the play script,
understanding so much is pre-given and all one
can do is to inflect a line or two in a particular
way, to inflict the pistol with one hand or two,
to drop one's head or hold it up, before moving
to the end, upstaged by the audience, and right.

The Birds of Harlem

The birds of Harlem are the birds
of America,
the brown nonentities
and the self-advertising glories.
They have returned from other lands
to a familiar bough
or the corner ledge of a brownstone.
To call them
the birds of Harlem
is to give airy nothings
a local habitation and a name.
It's a way of saying we belong
somewhere, a way of singing.

Seal

"History is dismantled music: slant,
bleak on gravel. One amasses silence,
another chastises silence with nettles,
stinging ferns. I oscillate in their jaws."

—Ishion Hutchinson, "Sibelius and Marley"

the sun was high the morning he bottomed
by a pool tastefully appointed with books
the all american with esquire good looks
bicycling out of the trousers and the prom

high too when he was tagged by two oreos
their cocks stuffing his sugar mouth and ass
highest when fucking the big tits stewardess
he brought ken so close he blows he blows

overdosed on prescription medicine
provided some say by a kindly client
by sean on screen by matt in life he went
he went and now the juicy worms have him

out of the datsun rocketing at 90
an ex vice mayor shoots his smallish wad
and so extends a southern lightning rod
for sneering lefties and godly righties

the obvious phallus of a congressman
stretching north his gray boxer briefs
he tweets to her for his obscure relief
the aphrodisiac of attention

there will be less and less for everyone
as billionaires decide what we will see
power and sex and ads for liberty
will divvy up the vision of the sun

today they coat the sun in candy crust
tomorrow what will they make safe and sweet
and sell it to the masses for a treat
yesterday they were pushing new stardust

beehives are trucked to wanton cornfield blue
assyrian refugees in flatbed ferries
when brooklyn bees are fed maraschino cherries
blood honey robitussin red for you

all is to be sold marrow pit and sap
it started long ago the gm tree
the apple once a bit of machinery
for our redemption is now an app

the sun will not stay long enough to broker
ceasefire in the latest games of death
the day is shot through with a dying breath
the coffee cold the croissant mediocre

i will catch some infection or another
from the untreated slash in someones head
a youtube video of an oyster bed
round razors laved and gleaming in fresh water

tracks my eyes and gurgles from my desk
not high up enough to deserve a window
the underling looks into the undertow
the numbers hide by changing as he asks

opening a crack of the eyeball to the sun
i am divided from the objects lit
even the violent corpse of this misfit
that i now raise as if rolling a stone

i dont know if it dies during the night
i do know when i wake that it is dead
the toaster oven revives the pita bread
an oversized knife will slice into bites

the coffee grinder now nearly unmanned
next week it will dispense with human quirk
woven from sweat that will not wear its work
the cotton shirt eviscerates my hands

the sun stretching out on the couch of clouds
complains of ennui and insomnia
the night is long but all too soon i hear
the coffins chewing up the crusty shrouds

i take my blackness out to walk the park
bitch owners let their petty dooms run wild
or train them to pick up a spotty child
so carefully the skin wont hear a mark

a little ruin runs across the street
mummy cries out stay buddy where you are
judging it love the bud runs back to her
and the three car pile up is complete

i have been barking at the sun the bone
that will not drop into my raving maw
until commissioned first to shock and awe
the bomb is tossed by a cruising drone

i have been watching porn and buying books
knowing a history of all my searches
so purely indicative of my urges
is open to the state and to its crooks

what shall i choose from the catalogue
the causes are so many and so urgent
defend the sloe impeach the president
the dialectic has mushroomed to dialogue

the foreskin of the sun a mottled black
laved by bonus tubes of antiseptic cream
the meatus passes an untreated stream
of bloodflecked pus and semi solid dreck

the bath drainer sprouts sticky clumps of hair
between my fingers the material
i rub and jack off to the smell of cells
shooting into the tiles a cross de guerre

the cracks between the eyes are filled with grout
the body lathered with the sweat of butter
from neck to haunch from inner thighs to outer
in the next room my husband rubs one out

the sun again is a big orange pill
stuck in the blue throat of the sky
pretty colors kind of plasticky
guaranteed to return a mans free will

we listen quietly to the rocking train
not making a sound if we can help it
the train is throwing a shrill hissy fit
we are quiet like a brown blood stain

the adderall is on extended release
im muzzling the bitch impulse to scream
the cost is not prohibitive per diem
the insulin shot into zolofts peace

sunday like any other day of the week
begins the work of filling up the time
the hours integral empty sublime
present so many unravished physiques

a white boy fifteen or sixteen of age
honey for hair runs past in tennis shorts
i unzip my jeans and take out my cock
behind the journal and uncrease a page

minutes later his older brother shows
bulging a crimson harvard arch sweatshirt
his rowboat legs pumping along the dirt
my dick hardens unbearably below

he comes again this time pushing a stroller
in front of him as he runs after his youth
thicker in the waist longer in the tooth
and jogging back and forth as if bipolar

the final figures are predictable
the crumpled suit the shaky gouty walk
i close my eyes and whack my wilting cock
the hours whirring by on bicycles

hurtling around the sun itself spinning
at dizzying speeds in differential circles
a wave of subatomic particles
dies on the bat in the day's last inning

that fine metallic ping in the spring air
draws in its wake a low approving roar
and then a vast communal silence soars
through the sound barrier bursting into cheers

around the field the muzak of the spheres
echoes in one wild dionysian pitch
until the noise reduces to a twitch
a bloody twitch is leaking from my ears

the system of the micro sun the net
is streaming nonstop videos of the blast
no one not one escapes from the broadcast
of rookie mayhem and the terror threat

someone sincere a would be hacktivist
has broken into the sys and gained access
to the rootkit ensconced in our recess
the terrorist works with other idealists

they want to combat code with better code
they say they will get whatever they phish for
they promise very soon all that we wish for
we will get too when we press download

without a doubt the sun from house to house
flushes out the subversive elements
brother betrays brother to the agents
the son drags forth the mother by her blouse

words fall in line behind the party line
or else escape with poppers underground
the suspects are required to walk around
with foreheads branded with a dollar sign

and when my usefulness is finally done
finally will come a knuckle on my door
at least i hope to be accounted for
by the incomparable agents of the sun

flying into the cut and pasted sun
a black hawk chopper twirls its razor blades
charlie brown is pouring lucys lemonade
over the muffled face of a boy tied down

no bots no movement in this corridor
constructed by an old drawing program
outside the photograph four videocams
monitor the white space above the floor

i cannot tear my eyes away for dread
a grin has opened in the continuum
a tree beckons with multiplying arms
this beady blackbird with a bluish head

a tiny wedge of the suns landing gear
is lodged between my military teeth
the chinese toothpick rescues bits of wreath
charred fat and streaky musculature

flossing day and night is of little use
the gum burying the bone bleeds and bleeds
but the updated body has to feed
on real estate and pomegranate juice

mouth striated with lost and found remains
i orate with a nasty piggish kink
to the blind glass above the bloody sink
morning breath smelling of smoking brains

bereft the last sun nearly dies of fright
i touch the pad the screen does not light up
black coffee drizzles from the paper cup
the store sells sexy underwear to tykes

amazon stocks eighty kinds of cereals
salted and unsalted and honeyed nuts
fruit of every hue on the color chart
packed close on ice the recycled mackerel

the bully crotches beg to be unzipped
forgot to get my favorite graham bread
our bots rechargeable battery dead
the arrows of the earth are iron tipped

the sun a bit of deep programming code
swivels its suspect electronic eye
logging on at hotspots to its wifi
i give away my bearings on the road

wired to love whats good i love
to stir my stick inside a mans shithole
and submit to the suns social control
though wired to fear what i know not of

a reproductive program gone rogue
at whiz school im still gainfully employed
to vaccinate the young by being paranoid
of what is in vain and what in vogue

the cancer sun of the computer screen
bathes now the dying flower of my face
the indices free fall in a coup de grace
or fly up tempting the empyrean

my teeth are rotting in their violent rant
a patch of bone has to be grafted on
to the jaw thats not altogether gone
to anchor the screw up of the implant

once running up and down a shitty alley
i did not think was any shitty then
i saw lift off a preacher man both hands
stabilizing a lily of the valley

. . . the morning sun the climbing rose
love in which i had placed all faith and hope
is in my hands a fraying piece of rope
affixed to nothing but the bodys throes

horizontal as custom and the bed
the days check into months check into years
commaed by wretched anniversaries
a run on sentence pricked in ball point red

into the rupture of a tight white ass
or the enormous pecs of a hot wet dream
so clean theres not an ounce of steel in him
old envy and its shining stooping face

the sun rises and the sun sets one day
the light unclenching its hold on the air
its noticeably colder everywhere
is that brad sinking into the subway

a boy is sucking up his third ice pop
his mother quizzing her tablet for updates
a robocop whizzes by on his skates
a bench where two old faggots had to stop

the mere, oily and epic, is on fire
the ducks swim calmly through the burning field
the envelope of day has been unsealed
of man and the long decline of empire

i woke from the great monkeys dream—
he who comes after me wakes from my dream

Acknowledgments

My deep gratitude to my dearest friends and best readers, Andrew Howdle, Helaine Smith, and Eric Norris, whose comments on a draft of this manuscript have again saved me from many blunders. Thank you. This volume is dedicated to Guy E. Humphrey, whose love saves me every day from myself.

The artworks described in "Art Show at the Center" are inspired by the works of Jessica Witte. https://jessicawitte.com/

I am grateful to the editors of the following journals for publishing these poems, sometimes in earlier versions:

Birmingham Poetry Review: "I Don't Believe in the Long Arc of Justice," "Elegy for Seal" ("Elegy"), "The Birds of Harlem"

CHA: "Counting Song"

Evergreen Review: ["the sun was high the morning he bottomed"], ["out of the datsun rocketing at 90'"], ["today they coat the sun in candy crust"], ["i have been barking at the sun the bone"], ["the system of the micro sun the net"], ["without a doubt the sun from house to house"], and ["flying into the cut and pasted sun"]

Mascara: "Strongman from Qinshi Huangdi's Tomb"

Softblow: "Nebraska," "Art Show at the Center," "A Tale of Two Cities, Three Maybe," "Arrival New York," "80's Dance Party on Throwback Thursday" ("Cheeks")

About the Poet

Jee Leong Koh is the author of *Steep Tea* (Carcanet), named a Best Book of the Year by UK's *Financial Times*, and a Finalist for the Lambda Literary Award. He has published three other books of poems, *Payday Loans* (Poets Wear Prada Press, Math Paper Press), *Equal to the Earth* (Bench Press), and *Seven Studies for a Self Portrait* (Bench Press), and a collection of zuihitsu, *The Pillow Book* (Math Paper Press, Awai Books), which was shortlisted for the Singapore Literature Prize. His work has been translated into Japanese, Chinese, Vietnamese, Malay, Spanish, Russian, and Latvian.

Jee lives in New York City. He is the founder of the literary non-profit Singapore Unbound, which organizes the biennial Singapore Literature Festival in New York City and the monthly Second Saturdays Reading Series, and publishes works of poetry, fiction, and creative non-fiction through Gaudy Boy.

About the Press

Sibling Rivalry Press is an independent press based in Little Rock, Arkansas. It is a sponsored project of Fractured Atlas, a nonprofit arts service organization. Contributions to support the operations of Sibling Rivalry Press are tax-deductible to the extent permitted by law, and your donations will directly assist in the publication of work that disturbs and enraptures. To contribute to the publication of more books like this one, please visit our website and click *donate*.

Sibling Rivalry Press gratefully acknowledges the following donors, without whom this book would not be possible:

Anonymous (18)
Arkansas Arts Council
John Bateman
W. Stephen Breedlove
Dustin Brookshire
Sarah Browning
Billy Butler
Asher Carter
Don Cellini
Nicole Connolly
Jim Cory
Risa Denenberg
John Gaudin
In Memory of Karen Hayes
Gustavo Hernandez
Amy Holman
Jessica Jacobs & Nickole Brown
Paige James
Nahal Suzanne Jamir
Allison Joseph
Collin Kelley
Trevor Ketner

Andrea Lawlor
Anthony Lioi
Ed Madden & Bert Easter
Mitchell, Blackstock, Ivers & Sneddon, PLLC
Stephen Mitchell
National Endowment for the Arts
Stacy Pendergrast
Simon Randall
Paul Romero
Randi M. Romo
Carol Rosenfeld
Joseph Ross
In Memory of Bill Rous
Matthew Siegel
Alana Smoot
Katherine Sullivan
Tony Taylor
Leslie Taylor
Hugh Tipping
Guy Traiber
Mark Ward
Robert Wright

CPSIA information can be obtained
at www.ICGtesting.com
Printed in the USA
FSHW021556160120
66014FS

9 781943 977758